PROJECT SCIENCE

LIGHT AND COLOR

Alan Ward

Franklin Watts

New York • London • Toronto • Sydney

© 1992 Franklin Watts

Franklin Watts, Inc.
95 Madison Avenue
New York, NY 10016

Library of Congress Cataloging-in-Publication Data

Ward, Alan, 1932-
     Light and color / by Alan Ward.
         p. cm. — (Project science)
     Includes index.
     Summary: Uses simple experiments and projects to demonstrate the
principles of light and color.
     ISBN 0-531-14231-0
     1. Light — Juvenile literature. 2. Light — Experiments — Juvenile
Literature. 3. Color — Juvenile literature. 4. Color — Experiments —
Juvenile literature. [1. Light — Experiments. 2. Color —
Experiments. 3. Experiments.] I. Title. II. Series: Ward, Alan,
1932-Project science.
     QC360.W37 1993
535'.078—dc20

92-5140
CIP
AC

Series Editor: A. Patricia Sechi
Design: Mike Snell
Illustrations: Ian Thompson
Typesetting: Spectrum, London

Printed in Great Britain

CONTENTS

4 Where does light come from?
6 Light waves
8 Reflected light
10 Mirrors
12 Making shadows
14 How to bend light
16 Upside down images
18 Colors of the spectrum
20 Mixing colors
22 Afterimages
24 Lights in the sky
26 Light entertainment
28 Extra projects
30 Glossary

WHERE DOES LIGHT COME FROM?

Most of our light comes from the sun. Before the electric light bulb was invented about 100 years ago, people used candles or burned gas to provide them with light. To save money many poor people went to bed at sunset and got up at sunrise.

Do you really know how much you depend on light and your sense of sight? You can prove it by trying to do the following things in the dark:

Telephone a friend

Change the battery in your flashlight

Figure out the value of a handful of coins

Write your name

Put laces in a shoe

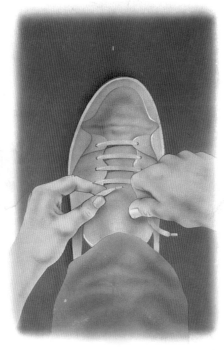

Sew on a button

Draw a pig

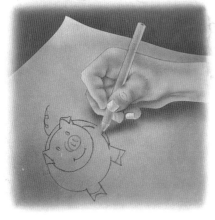

How well did you manage to do these things? Try to find your way about the house while blindfolded.

Day and night

The sun does not travel around the earth. It only looks as if it does. The sun seems to rise in one part of the sky, then move across it and set in another part of the sky. In fact, it is the earth which is turning. It turns all the way around every 24 hours.

When the sun is shining in the morning, take the tennis ball into a room that has a south-facing window. Draw the curtains, leaving a gap between them about 10 inches wide. Close any other curtains so that the room is as dark as possible.

Stand sideways next to the window and hold the ball

near the gap between the curtains. The ball is the planet Earth. The side facing the sun is well lit; this is "daytime." The other side of the ball is "nighttime."

Now turn the ball in your hands. Notice that each part of the ball is in light (daytime) or dark (nighttime) as it turns.

**WARNING
Never look directly at the sun. This is a very dangerous thing to do.** The light from the sun is very strong and can easily damage your eyes. Never look at the sun through a magnifying glass, telescope, or binoculars.

Stand with your back to the sun and pretend that you are the planet Earth. Keep turning on the spot slowly, (going to your left which is counterclockwise). Notice the sun appearing on your left. This is the "sunrise." Keep turning and the sun appears to move from left to right, before disappearing on your right — at sunset.

LIGHT WAVES

Light is a form of energy. Like tiny waves, it ripples out from its source. This source can be the sun, a flame, or even a television — anything that gives out light by itself.

Light travels in straight lines

Light waves spreading out from a light source are called radiation. They travel in straight lines. When the waves form narrow beams of light they are called light rays. You may have seen the thin beams of light in a laser light show.

Make sure you use a flashlight with a strong beam. Tie the string around a tree trunk and hold the long end in your hand. Walk away from the tree until the string is pulled tight. Now shine the flashlight down the piece of string toward the tree. The straight piece of string will help to remind you that light usually travels in straight lines.

YOU NEED:

- a flashlight
- a long piece of string

Did you know?

It takes about 8.5 minutes for light from the sun to reach us on Earth. In the time it takes you to blink, light can travel all the way around the earth. It is hard to imagine the speed at which light travels, but it is actually 186,000 miles per second. Try and figure out how far away the sun is from the earth.

Light bounces

In some ways light waves are like streams of rubber balls that can bounce off things. The tiny waves are invisible until they get inside your eyes. Light waves bounce off people and objects, such as flowers, and then enter your eyes. The light from the objects, which seem to shine, is reflected into your eyes, enabling you to see.

Memories and dreams

Close your eyes and try to remember the pictures that appear on this page. Do you have a kind of view of things inside your head?

What has happened?

It is by the power of light that "pictures" appear inside your head. At night, while you dream, the brain plays tricks with these images, or "picture memories," and you have adventures in your mind's dream world.

REFLECTED LIGHT

When you look in a mirror, light bounces off you onto the mirror. The light is reflected off your face and then travels straight to the mirror, where it is reflected back into your eyes. But to your eyes and brain, it seems as if the light is coming from inside the mirror. It looks like a sort of "phantom" you behind the glass.

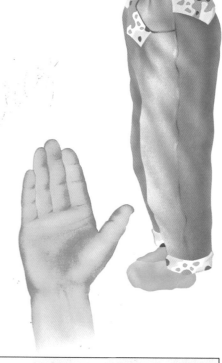

Hold up the palms of your hands and look at them carefully. Your face and its reflection in the mirror are alike in the same way that your two palms are alike. Your reflection is like a palm print, where left and right are reversed.

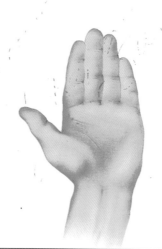

Mirror monsters

You can use a mirror to make some scary-looking monsters. Here's how.

YOU NEED:

- pictures of faces (use old photographs or newspaper and magazine cuttings)
- a small rectangular mirror

Place the mirror halfway across the picture in either a horizontal or a vertical direction, so that half of the face is reflected in the mirror. Notice what the whole face looks like now. It is very different from the original picture!

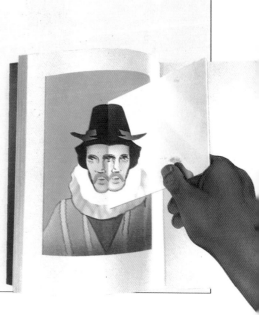

Did you know?

The left and right sides of your face are different. You can see this for yourself by standing in front of a large mirror. Hold a rectangular mirror lengthwise down the center of your face so that one half of your face is reflected in the mirror. Can you recognize yourself in the big mirror now?

Flat and curved mirrors

Take a look at your reflection in the mirror in your bathroom. Have you ever looked at your reflection in the side of a polished kettle or a shiny hubcap on a car? It is not the same as the one in the bathroom mirror.

What has happened?

Most of the mirrors that hang in your house are made from a flat sheet of glass with a coating of metal on the back. When you look at yourself in these mirrors, you see a reflection that is the same shape and size as you are. But the side of a kettle or a hubcap are curved surfaces. Like curved mirrors, they alter your reflection so that it is not the same shape or size as you are. The inside and outside surfaces of bubbles are also examples of curved mirror reflectors.

MIRRORS

A mirror changes the direction in which light waves travel by reflecting them back to your eyes. If you place a mirror at an angle, you can use it to see around corners. In the same way, the light waves will be reflected from the mirror into your eyes.

Making a periscope

Tape the lid onto the box all the way around. Stand the box on one end and cut 2 slots in opposite sides of the box as shown. Fit the mirrors into the slots, one above the other. The mirrors should be fixed at an angle of 45 degrees (this is the angle you get by folding a paper square in half).

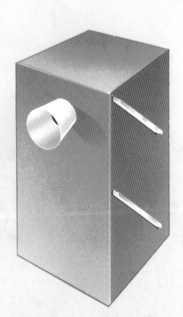

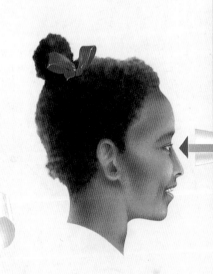

Cut circles out of the sides of the box exactly opposite the reflective surfaces of the mirrors. Push a yogurt cup into each hole. Point the top opening at an object on the other side of the room. The light from this object will be reflected down through the box and out to your eye. You can use your periscope to look over walls and around corners.

Did you know?

Magicians use mirrors to help them in many of their tricks. Have you seen a magician make a rabbit appear in an empty box? Do you know how this is done?

Yes, by using mirrors. When the front of the box is opened, it looks empty. The sloping mirror reflects the bottom of the box, making the space behind the mirror look empty. But in fact the rabbit is hidden behind the mirror. Then the magician closes the door, he shouts "Abracadabra" and then opens the top of the box and pulls out the rabbit.

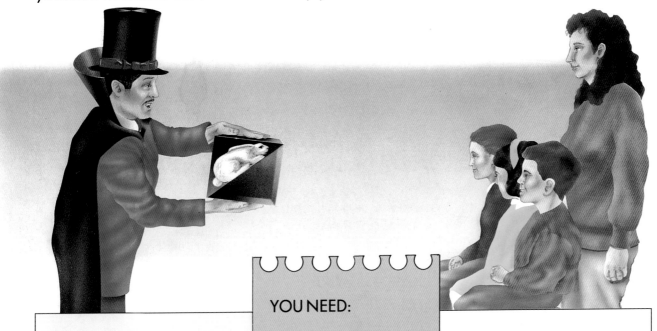

Making a kaleidoscope

Using the tape, join the two mirrors together along two long edges. Open up the mirrors like a book and stand them up on a table. Put some flowers between them. What do you see? Try making patterns with other objects such as leaves, beads, small toys, string, or a crumpled handkerchief.

YOU NEED:

- two mirrors (they should be the same size)
- tape

MAKING SHADOWS

If light cannot pass through a material or object, we say that the material is opaque. If light rays are only partly blocked by a material, or they are bent by it and become mixed up on their way through, we say that the material is translucent. This means that you can see some light through it. Wax paper and frosted glass are translucent materials. And if you can look right through a material such as clear glass, then it is called transparent.

Notice how light rays from a well-lit room stream through a gap in the doorway and travel across a dark hallway. The edges of the beam of light are straight.

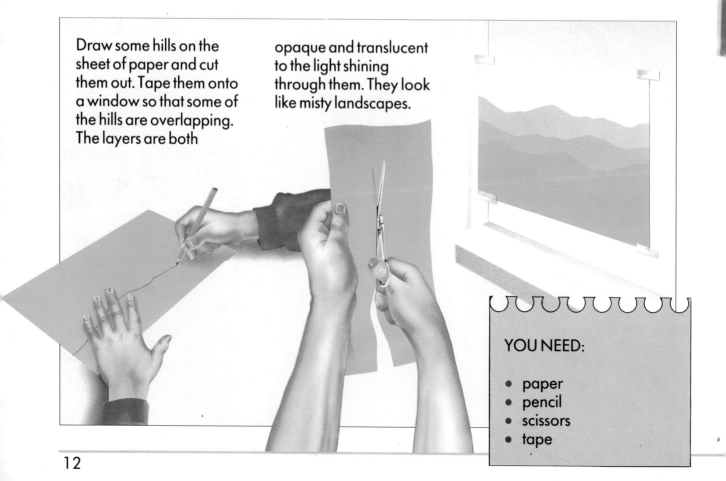

Draw some hills on the sheet of paper and cut them out. Tape them onto a window so that some of the hills are overlapping. The layers are both opaque and translucent to the light shining through them. They look like misty landscapes.

YOU NEED:

- paper
- pencil
- scissors
- tape

Did you know?

The other name for a sundial is a shadow clock. Look for a sundial in a park or garden and see if you can figure out how to tell the time by it. See what different kinds of shadows you can get with a hoop or an umbrella.

Shadow fun

Do you know how shadows are made? Have you ever seen someone using their hands to make animal shadows on a wall? A hand-shadow expert can make shadow pictures of rabbits, monkeys, and even dragons. Can you do this?

If you wake up in the night, try going into a dark room where there is a video recorder switched on, with its small light glowing. Your super-sensitive eyes will see a giant shadow of yourself. This is made by rays from the recorder's tiny light.

With the help of two friends, make a six-armed shadow monster. You can do this in sunlight or by using a lamp. See if your shadow hands, not your real ones, can shake hands. Find out if your shadow is ever exactly the same height as you are. Is your shadow dwarflike, or is it like a thin giant?

What has happened?

You get a shadow when light rays are blocked and cannot travel any farther. The shadow shows you the outline of the object that is blocking the path of the light rays. The shadow of an opaque object, such as a stone or a book, is black.

Did you know?

In Southeast Asia people enjoy watching shadow puppet plays. The puppets are flat cutout shapes that are mounted on sticks. They have jointed parts that are moved by rods. The puppets are held next to a white sheet with a light behind it.

HOW TO BEND LIGHT

Light rays travel through the air in straight lines. Whenever light rays pass from a transparent material to another transparent material that is either thicker (denser) or thinner (less dense), the light rays are bent. We say that the rays are refracted.

YOU NEED:

- a video cassette slipcase
- white paper
- a small plastic magnifying glass
- tape
- a hair comb

Cover one side of the slipcase with white paper. Using the tape, attach the magnifying glass at one end of the side covered with paper. Half of the magnifying glass's lens must be sticking up over the edge of the slipcase.

Hold the slipcase in one hand and point it at the sun. **Remember not to look directly at the sun.**

Hold the comb on the side of the lens facing the sun. Move the comb and slipcase until the rays of light are coming through the comb's teeth and falling onto the white paper.

What has happened? The light rays that do not pass through the lens fall on the paper in straight lines. But those rays which pass through the lens of the magnifying glass are refracted. They meet at a point on the other side of the lens.

Did you know?

On the bottom of some heavy glasses, such as tumblers, you may notice that the glass is thinner in the middle. Try looking at your finger through this kind of "lens." What do you see?

YOU NEED:

- a glass of water
- a straw
- a small plastic bath toy

Water tricks

Put your finger into the glass of water and then look at it through the glass. Does it still look the same? Have you ever taken a pickled onion out of a jar and been surprised?

Now put a ruler in the water. Move it around and look at it from different positions. It does not always look the same. See what a straw looks like in a glass of water.

Hold the plastic bath toy on the other side of the glass and look at it through the glass of water. You can make the duck look as if it is pointing in the other direction. If you find this a bit difficult, try shutting one eye.

What has happened?

Just as the plastic lens in the magnifying glass refracted the light rays, so water does the same thing. When light rays enter your eyes, your brain senses that they are coming from different places. This explains why things look different, for example bigger, smaller, or the wrong way around.

15

UPSIDE DOWN IMAGES

In the days before the camera or movies and television were invented, wealthy people entertained their friends with a moving picture light show. There was just one problem with this kind of show — the pictures were upside down!

The audience sat in a special room with only one window. The window was blacked out, except for a small hole. The room was painted black, except for a plain white wall opposite the window. The room's owner, as well as the guests, then watched the white wall. They secretly saw everything happening in the garden outside the room. Do you know how?

What has happened?
This type of room was called a *camera obscura*, meaning a darkened chamber, and it led to the invention of the photographic camera. Light rays traveled from objects outside in the sunshine, such as trees, hills, or animals. The rays entered the room through the small hole in the blackened window, where they crossed over before continuing onto the white wall, which acted as a screen. Because the rays had crossed, the image of the object outside was projected upside down onto the wall.

You should be able to get a box from your local grocery store or supermarket. Make sure that it isn't damaged. Fold over the open end of the box and tape the sides together. Also tape down any other loose flaps, to keep out the light. You can make your box even more lightproof by taping on the black paper where necessary. Plug any holes in the corners with the modeling clay. If you want, you can paint the inside of the box with the black paint.

At one end of the box, cut a hole big enough for your head to poke through. Make sure the hole is to one side of the middle. Use the darning needle to prick a small neat hole in the end of the box where your head will go, but make sure that your head will not block the hole. Cover the opposite end of the box with white paper to make a screen.

Take the box outside on a bright day. Poke your head in the box. You can tie a scarf around your neck to make the box more lightproof. Position the small hole so that it is pointing at something interesting.

Now look at the screen inside your box. You will see brilliant moving pictures. It's like being

inside a *camera obscura* or a modern photographic camera, where the picture on the camera's film would also be upside down.

Did you know?
Photography is the art of creating images on film, using light. If the screen in your model *camera obscura* were a film made of light-sensitive paper, it would be possible to take a photograph. But you would need to keep the camera still for a long time.

COLORS OF THE SPECTRUM

The light from the sun, and the light from a table lamp, seem to be white. But sunlight and electric light are really made up of a band of different colors. This band of colors is called the spectrum.

YOU NEED:

- a small mirror
- a shallow dish filled with water
- modeling clay
- white paper
- tape

Water prism

Choose a windowsill that is sunny in the mornings. Place the dish of water on the windowsill and slant the mirror at one end of the dish. You can stick the mirror in position with a small piece of modeling clay. Make sure that the mirror is facing the morning sunshine. Now tape a sheet of white paper on the window. Move the dish and the mirror until you can see a band of brilliant colors on the sheet of paper.

What has happened?

The sunlight travels to the wedge-shaped section of water above the slanted mirror. The "wedge" of water acts like a prism. A prism is usually made of a triangular-shaped piece of glass. It can separate white light (sunlight) into different colors. The water prism has split the sunlight into the seven colors of the spectrum: red, orange, yellow, green, blue, indigo, and violet. These are the same as the colors of the rainbow.

Did you know?

When you see a rainbow in the sky, you are really seeing the reflections from millions and millions of raindrops. Each acts like a water prism, separating the sun's light into its different colors.

Why do things have colors?

Light waves consist of ripples that are a different length for every color. Each kind of wave produces a different color sensation inside your brain. When all the different-colored light waves are mixed together in the sunlight, they make white light.

Chemicals called pigments absorb, or soak in, certain color ripples. They allow other color ripples to bounce off them, or be reflected. A yellow pigment absorbs all kinds of color wave, except those that we sense as yellow. A yellow pigment will reflect the waves of yellow light.

Sunflowers contain yellow pigment which reflects the yellow light into our eyes, and so the sunflower appears to be yellow. Leaves reflect green light. If they also reflect some yellow light, then we see them as yellowish or pale green leaves.

Did you know?

A newspaper looks white because it reflects most of the light waves that fall onto it. But the black pigment absorbs almost all light waves. It does not reflect any colors and so we cannot really count black as a color.

MIXING COLORS

When you look at the picture on a television screen, you can see all the colors of the rainbow. But if you look very closely at the screen, you will see that the picture is actually made up of dots or dashes in just three colors: red, green, and blue. The "rainbow" colors of your television are an illusion.

The red, green, and blue spots can shine brightly, dimly, or not at all, to provide the right mixture for the colors needed for the "living" pictures. The colors on the television screen are mixtures of actual lights.

Try mixing different paint colors for yourself, and see what colors you can make. You will be mixing pigments. Don't forget the white pigment, which can reflect the light waves that produce all the colors.

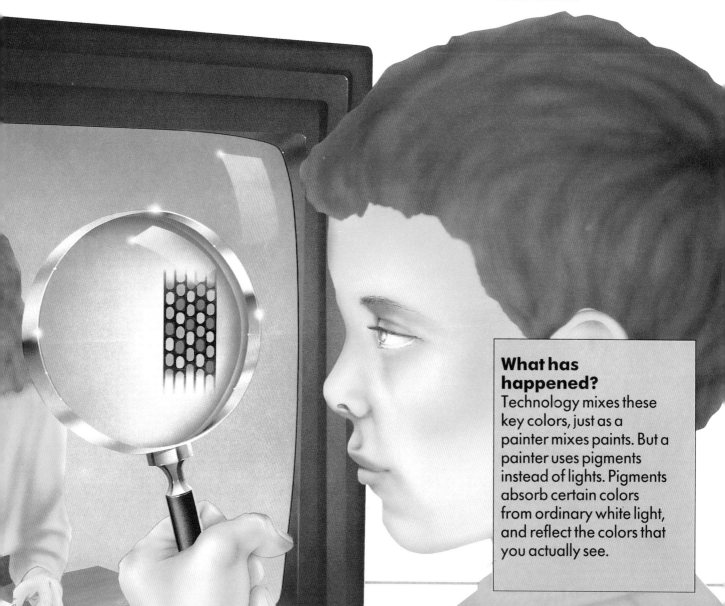

What has happened?

Technology mixes these key colors, just as a painter mixes paints. But a painter uses pigments instead of lights. Pigments absorb certain colors from ordinary white light, and reflect the colors that you actually see.

Mixing lights

Make a cardboard disk by drawing around the cup and cutting out the circle shape. Divide the cardboard into seven sections of equal size. Color each section a different color of the rainbow: red, orange, yellow, green, blue, indigo, and violet.

Cut out a second disk and divide this one into three equal sections. Color these red, green, and blue. Push a pencil stub through the center of each disk, to make them into spinning tops. When you spin your tops, all their colors will be reflected into your eyes by the white daylight. You will see that spinning blurs the colors to a dirty white.

Remember that you are using pigments and not pure lights to color your tops. But you can still see that mixtures of lights, can make the color white.

YOU NEED:

- white cardboard
- a cup
- a pencil
- scissors
- colored felt-tipped pens
- pencil stubs

Try making some other tops and coloring them in different ways. The colors that you see on your spinning tops are different from the colors made by the same mixture of paints.

Did you know?

You can mix colored lights quite easily for yourself. Tape different colored sheets of cellophane over the lenses of several flashlights. Mix the colored lights by shining their beams onto white paper.

AFTERIMAGES

The parts of our eyes and brain that see colors can sometimes cause our eyes to play tricks.

Try staring at a bunch of yellow flowers, such as daffodils or yellow chrysanthemums, while you count up to 20 slowly. Then stare at a blank sheet of white paper. What do you see? You should see a patch of purple on the paper and yet you know that the paper is white. You are seeing something that is not really there — a "ghost" image. Now try the same test with some purple flowers. The afterimage that you will see is yellow.

Time how long it takes your eyes to work properly again.

What has happened?

Your eyes are sensitive to three colors: red, green, and blue. The yellow light from the white mixture of daylight is reflected by the yellow flowers. This yellow light is made up of light waves containing red and green light.

When you look hard at a yellow object, it tires the parts of your eyes that you use for seeing red and green. They get so tired that they stop working properly and take a rest. When you stare at the white paper it reflects all the colors present in white daylight. But only the parts of your eyes that see the color blue are working properly. That is why you seem to be seeing a blue ghost of the yellow flowers.

A spooky ghost show

Here are some more colored shapes to haunt you. Stare at each one for 20 seconds and then look for the ghost in the white space beside it. You can draw and color your own set of ghosts. Ask your friends to try out your spooky ghost show.

Did you know?

These "ghosts" are called afterimages and they help to explain some ghostly sightings in real life. At night when white owls are lit by street lights they can look like ghosts. Trees also seem to have frightening shapes when you look at them in the dark. Even laundry left out on a clothesline might give you a scare at night.

LIGHTS IN THE SKY

The sun is the brightest star in the sky. It is the main source of heat and light in the solar system. The solar system includes the sun and the nine planets, one of which is Earth.

In the daytime the sky is filled with stars, but they are too faint for us to notice them in the sunlight. In the same way you often do not notice that a light is switched on in a brightly sunlit room. In cities and towns it is sometimes difficult to see and enjoy the stars even at night because of the glare in the sky caused by many types of lighting, such as street lights.

Stargazing

Ask an adult to take you out on a nighttime "star watch." This is best done in a wide open or country area, away from the bright lights of more built-up areas.
Pick out a star that appears to be directly above a landmark, such as a tree or fence. Now keep still and wait. If you are patient, you will notice the star moving. But in fact it's really you who are moving, as the earth turns slowly around.
Try to identify some famous star families, called constellations, such as Orion (the Hunter) and Taurus (the Bull). A group of stars called the Plow lies in the constellation of the Great Bear (Ursa Major). Two of the Plow's stars point directly to Polaris (the North Star). This is one of the brightest stars in the Northern Hemisphere and it would be directly overhead if you were standing at the North Pole.

If you live in the Southern Hemisphere, try looking for a constellation called the Southern Cross. The longer arm of this group of stars points directly to the South Pole of the sky.

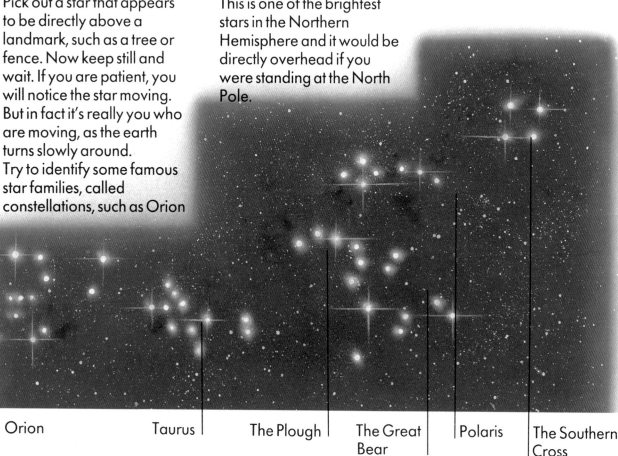

Orion   Taurus   The Plough   The Great Bear   Polaris   The Southern Cross

Did you know?

Other "night lights" in the sky include comets, meteors, and artificial satellites sent up into space. Comets are mostly made of thin gases that reflect sunlight. Meteors are rocks from outer space. They travel at high speed and as they rub against the air in the atmosphere, they become very hot and glow, giving off light. We somethimes call them "shooting stars."
Artificial satellites that are

launched into space do not give off a strong light of their own. Instead they reflect the light from the sun.

The moon's phases

Each month, the moon appears to change shape at different times of the month. These "changing shapes" of the moon are called phases.

When the moon is visible in the sky during a morning or late afternoon, stand facing it. Hold up the tennis ball in one hand. Now compare the shape of the moon with the shape of the light patch that you see on your tennis ball.

YOU NEED:

- a tennis ball

What has happened?

The moon travels around the earth about once every month. It also travels around the sun. Although the moon seems to give out lots of light, this is not light from the moon itself. The moon reflects light from the sun. The shape of the moon that we see from Earth depends on how much of the moon's surface is lit by the sun.

When there is a new moon, the moon is between the sun and the earth and we cannot see it. The moon's unlit part is invisible from the earth.

LIGHT ENTERTAINMENT

If you look around you carefully at the world of plants and animals, you may see some of the surprising things that light can do.

Light and nature

Have you ever walked through a forest or wooded area on a sunny day? Although you cannot see the sky because it is blocked off by the trees that meet over your head, sunlight still manages to filter through onto the forest floor. The leaves of the trees are translucent, so they allow the light to pass through them.

An insect, called a water strider, rests on the surface film of a stream. Its dry feet make tiny lens-shaped dimples in the water. These dimples behave like water lenses. They refract, or bend, the light outward, to form strange blotlike shadows. The edges of the shadows seem to be surrounded with golden halos where the sunlight is being focused.

Colored lights

Cut an eyehole at one end of the box lid. Cut out a large rectangular slot at the other end of the lid. Tape a sheet of colored cellophane over the slot.

Put different colored objects, such as a toy car inside the box. Look through the eyehole and see how the object changes color. Now try changing the color of the cellophane and you will see a different color light in your box.

The cellophane is transparent because it allows the light to pass through it. Transparent materials that control the color of the light passing through them are called filters.

YOU NEED:

- an empty shoe box
- scissors
- colored cellophane (use old candy wrappers)
- tape
- various household objects and small toys

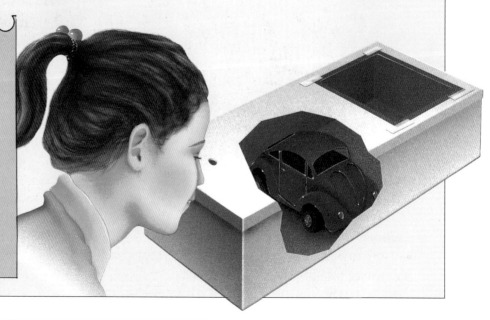

Color magic

Draw around the saucer to make a circle on the white paper. Copy the pattern of the disk shown here and cut out the circle. Paste it onto the cardboard and push the pencil through the center.

Spin your disk in strong light. You know that the disk is black and white, yet you can see different colors. What colors are they? The flicker effect produced by the spinning pattern makes your eyes send tiny signals to your brain. Your brain senses these signals as if they came from colored light.

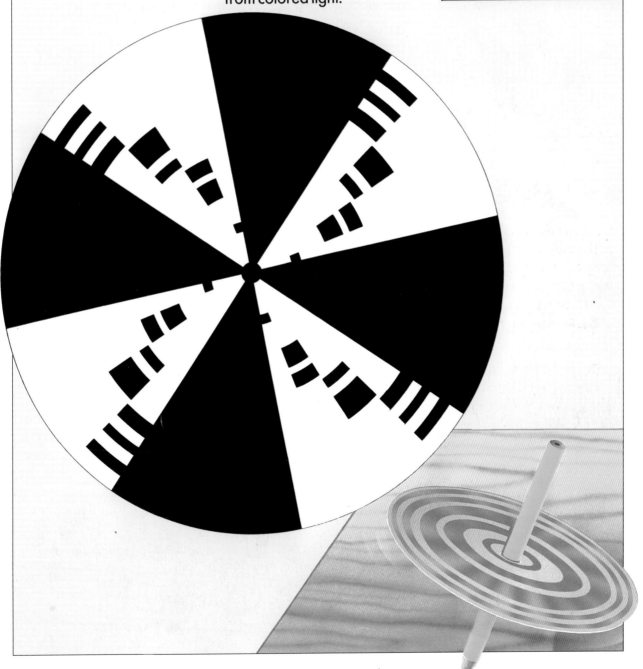

27

EXTRA PROJECTS

Shaping water into a lens

Ask an adult to cut two large holes in the side of an old unwanted bucket. Stretch the sheet of plastic over the top and tie it on with the string.

Now pour some water on top of the sheet. The weight of the water stretches the plastic into a lens shape. Place a coin on the palm of your hand and look at it through your water lens. What does it look like now? Try looking at other objects in the same way.

Construction paper photography

Place the different objects on the construction paper and leave the paper in strong summer sunlight. The areas of the paper that are not covered are "exposed." They are faded by the energy from the sunlight. Darker shadow shapes of the objects will be left on the unexposed areas. This is a very simple form of photography.

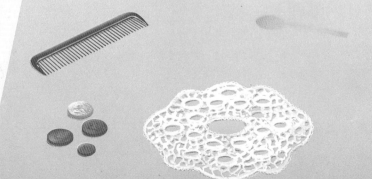

Make a blue sky!

A clear plastic bag filled with air does not look blue, yet the air-filled sky is blue. Read on to discover why.

Fill a glass with water and put it on a sheet of white paper. Place the glass so that the sun is shining on it. Add drops of milk to the water until the water looks bluish.

YOU NEED:

- a glass jar
- water
- white paper
- milk

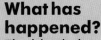

What has happened?

The blue light waves in sunlight are the shortest ones. Tiny particles and dust in the atmosphere reflect and scatter these blue rays more than any other rays. So they seem to be coming from all over the sky, making it appear blue. The drops of milk act like the particles and dust in the air, making the water in the jar look blue.

Shadow plays

You can make your own puppets and use them to perform a shadow play.

YOU NEED:

- cardboard
- scissors
- colored cellophane
- plant support sticks
- tape

Cut small holes in the cardboard and cover them with the cellophane to add some color to your show.

Put a sheet across a doorway and ask an adult to set up a lamp with a 100-watt light bulb behind the sheet. Make sure the bulb is not touching the sheet. The light will cast shadows of your puppets onto the sheet.

GLOSSARY

A

absorb
To soak in

C

camera obscura
A small dark room, inside which an upside down image of the scene outside is projected through a tiny hole.

constellation
A small group, or family, of stars. Each constellation has its own name, such as Ursa Major (Great Bear).

D

dense
Describes the "thickness" of any material or substance. Water is more dense than air, but less dense than glass.

E

energy
The mysterious power that makes things work. Light energy can change

chemicals (as in photography) and can also produce electricity (as in a solar cell).

F

focus
To bring light rays to a meeting point

I

illusion
An event that tricks your brain into seeing something that is not real.

image
A clear picture that is produced by light.

K

kaleidoscope
A device that makes changing patterns by repeated reflections in mirrors.

L

lens
A piece of transparent

material, such as glass or plastic, which refracts light rays to form an image.

light source
A glowing body that gives out its own light. The sun, other stars, a flame, and a light bulb are different kinds of light sources.

light waves
Tiny invisible ripples of energy that spread out in all directions from a light source. They produce the sensation of sight when they enter your eyes.

O

opaque
Describes any material that completely blocks light.

P

periscope
A device that is used for seeing around corners and for looking up over or under things. Mirrors inside the periscope reflect light.

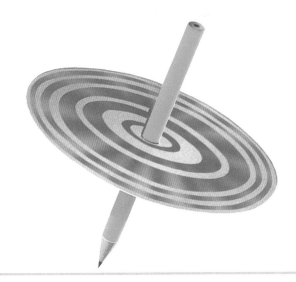

phase of the moon
The changing shape of the sunlit side of the moon, as we see it from the earth.

photography
Making pictures by letting light form images on a film. The film is coated with chemicals that are changed by light energy.

pigment
A substance that absorbs some light but also reflects the light that you sense as color.

prism
A device that splits light into separate groups of waves that can be sensed as different colors. Prisms are usually wedge-shaped and made of a transparent material such as glass. A prism can split white light into seven colors: red, orange, yellow, green, blue, indigo and violet.

R

reflect
To bounce off a surface. Mirrors reflect light waves.

refract
To bend or change direction. Light waves are refracted when they pass between transparent materials (air, glass, water) that have different densities.

S

satellite
A moon that keeps traveling around a planet along a path called an orbit. Scientists use modern technology to build artificial satellites and launch them into space.

shadow
A dark patch on a surface, caused by little or no light falling on the surface.

solar
To do with the sun. Energy from the sun is called solar energy.

spectrum
A band of colors that is produced on a screen when white light passes through a prism.

T

translucent
Describes a material that allows light to pass through it, but mixes up the passing rays and absorbs some of them. You cannot see clearly through translucent materials.

transparent
Describes a material that you can see through clearly. Windows are usually transparent.

INDEX

afterimage 22-23
artificial satellite 25,30

black 19
Bull, the 24

camera 16, 17
camera obscura 16, 17, 30
color 18-19, 20-21, 29
    mixing 20-21
    seeing 19, 20-21, 22-23,
      26-27
comet 25
constellation 24, 30

day 5, 24
dream 7

earth 5, 24, 25
electric light 4, 18
eye 5, 22

filter 26
focus 30

ghost (project) 23
glass 12, 15, 18
Great Bear, the 24

hand shadow 13
Hunter, the 24

image 16-17, 30
    afterimage 22-23

kaleidoscope 11, 30

laser 6
lens 14, 15, 30
    project 28
light 6, 14
    color of 18-19, 20-21
    rays 6, 12, 13, 14, 15, 16
    reflected 7, 8-11, 19,

20, 22, 25, 31
    refracted 14-15, 26, 31
    sources 4, 6, 24, 25, 30
    speed 7
    waves 6-7, 10, 19, 22,
      29, 30
light bulb 4

magician 11
meteor 25
mirror 8-9, 10-11
moon 25

night 5, 24
North Star, the 24

opaque 12, 13, 30
Orion 24

periscope 10, 30
phases of the moon 25, 31
photography 16, 17, 31
    project 28
pigment 19, 20, 31
    mixing colors 20, 21
Plow, the 24
Polaris 24
prism 18, 31

radiation 6
rainbow 18, 19
reflected light 7, 25, 31
    colors 19, 20, 22, 29
    mirrors 8-9, 10-11
refracted light 14-15, 26, 31

satellite 25, 31
seeing 4, 7, 8, 15
    around corners 10
    color 19, 20-21, 22-23
      26-27
shadow 12-13, 26, 31
shadow clock 13
shadow puppet 13

project 29
shooting star 25
sky, color of 29
solar system 24
Southern Cross 24
spectrum 18, 31
speed of light 7
star 24
sun 4, 5, 6, 24, 25
sundial 13
sunflower 19
sunlight 4, 5, 7, 26
    colors in 18-19, 29
    dangers of 5
sunrise 4, 5
sunset 4, 5

Taurus 24
television 6, 20
translucent 12, 26, 31
transparent 12, 14, 26, 31

upside down image 16-17
Ursa Major 24

water 15, 19, 28
water strider 26
waves, of light 6-7 10, 30
    and color 19, 22, 29
white light 18, 19, 20, 21, 22